YOUTUBE MILLIONAIRE BLUEPRINT

Build Your Empire Online

Joe Ilunjo

Copyright © 2024 Joe Ilunjo

All rights reserved

No part of this book may be reproduced, or stored in a retrieval system, or transmitted in any form or by any means, electronic, mechanical, photocopying, recording, or otherwise, without express written permission of the publisher.

ISBN-13: 979-8-3413-8426-2

CONTENTS

Title Page
Copyright
Chapter 1: The YouTube Gold Rush   1
Chapter 2: Building Your YouTube Foundation   7
Chapter 3: Content Creation Strategies   12
Chapter 4: Mastering YouTube Analytics   16
Chapter 5: Monetization Methods Beyond AdSense   20
Chapter 6: Building a Loyal Community   25
Chapter 7: Collaborations and Networking   30
Chapter 8: Scaling Your YouTube Business   36
Chapter 9: Advanced Monetization Techniques   42
Chapter 10: From YouTuber to Millionaire   47
About The Author   51

CHAPTER 1: THE YOUTUBE GOLD RUSH

Points Covered
1. Introduction
2. Understanding the Current YouTube Landscape
2.1. Platform Growth and User Base
2.2. Content Diversity
2.3. Technological Advancements
3. Recognizing the Financial Potential of the Platform
3.1. Advertising Revenue
3.2. Sponsorships and Brand Deals
3.3. Merchandise and Product Sales
3.4. Crowdfunding and Donations
4. Debunking Myths about YouTube Success
4.1. Overnight Success
4.2. Only Certain Types of Content Succeed
4.3. You Need Expensive Equipment
4.4. It's Too Late to Start
5. Conclusion

1. Introduction

YouTube has become a powerhouse in the world of online content creation and consumption. This chapter explores the current state of YouTube, its financial potential, and common misconceptions about achieving success on the platform. By understanding these aspects, aspiring content creators can position themselves to take advantage of the opportunities YouTube offers.

2. Understanding the Current YouTube Landscape

2.1. Platform Growth and User Base

YouTube's growth since its inception in 2005 has been nothing short of remarkable. Today, it boasts over 2 billion logged-in monthly users, making it the second most visited website globally. This massive user base presents an incredible opportunity for content creators to reach a wide audience.

The platform's reach extends across demographics, with users of all ages and backgrounds regularly engaging with content. This diversity allows creators to find and grow niche audiences, no matter how specific their content may be.

2.2. Content Diversity

One of YouTube's strengths is the sheer variety of content available. From educational videos and tutorials to entertainment and vlogs, there's something for everyone. This diversity means that creators have the freedom to produce content that aligns with their passions and expertise.

Popular content categories include:
- How-to and DIY videos
- Product reviews
- Gaming content
- Music videos and covers
- Comedy sketches
- Educational content
- Vlogs and personal stories

The platform's algorithm is designed to help users discover new content, which means that even smaller creators have the opportunity to grow their audience over time.

2.3. Technological Advancements

YouTube continually evolves, introducing new features and improvements to enhance the user experience. Recent advancements include:

- Improved video quality, supporting up to 8K resolution
- Live streaming capabilities
- 360-degree video support
- Virtual reality content
- Shorts, YouTube's answer to short-form video content

These technological improvements provide creators with more tools to produce engaging content and connect with their audience in new and exciting ways.

3. Recognizing the Financial Potential of the Platform

3.1. Advertising Revenue

The YouTube Partner Program (YPP) allows creators to monetize their content through ads. Once a channel meets the eligibility requirements (1,000 subscribers and 4,000 watch hours in the past 12 months), creators can start earning money from ads displayed on their videos.

Ad revenue can vary widely depending on factors such as:

- Number of views
- Video length
- Viewer engagement
- Ad type
- Niche and target audience

While earnings start small, successful creators can earn substantial amounts through ad revenue alone.

3.2. Sponsorships and Brand Deals

As channels grow, they often attract the attention of brands looking to reach their audience. Sponsorships and brand deals can be incredibly lucrative, often surpassing ad revenue for many creators.

These partnerships can take various forms:
- Sponsored videos
- Product placements
- Affiliate marketing
- Brand ambassadorships

The key to securing these deals is building a loyal and engaged audience that aligns with a brand's target market.

3.3. Merchandise and Product Sales

Many successful YouTubers expand their income streams by selling merchandise or their own products. This can include:
- Branded clothing and accessories
- Digital products (e.g., ebooks, courses)
- Physical products related to their niche

YouTube provides tools to help creators sell merchandise directly through their channel, making it easier to turn viewers into customers.

3.4. Crowdfunding and Donations

Some creators choose to leverage their audience's support through crowdfunding platforms or direct donations. Options include:
- Patreon for ongoing support
- Ko-fi for one-time donations
- YouTube's Super Chat feature during live streams

This approach works particularly well for creators who produce content that their audience finds valuable and wants to support directly.

4. Debunking Myths about YouTube Success

4.1. Myth: Overnight Success

Reality: While some videos do go viral, sustainable success on YouTube typically requires consistent effort over time. Most successful creators spend months or years building their audience before seeing significant growth.

Key factors for long-term success include:
- Consistent upload schedule
- Continuous improvement in content quality
- Engaging with the audience
- Adapting to platform changes and trends

4.2. Myth: Only Certain Types of Content Succeed

Reality: While some content categories may be more popular overall, there are successful channels in virtually every niche. The key is to create content that resonates with a specific audience, even if it's not mainstream.

Success stories exist in diverse fields such as:
- Niche hobbies
- Specialized professional skills
- Local culture and traditions
- Unique personal experiences

4.3. Myth: You Need Expensive Equipment

Reality: While high-quality equipment can enhance content, it's not a requirement for success. Many successful creators started with basic equipment, focusing on content quality and audience engagement.

Essential elements for success include:
- Compelling content
- Consistency
- Audience interaction
- Authentic presentation

As a channel grows, reinvesting in better equipment can improve production quality, but it's not necessary to start.

4.4. Myth: It's Too Late to Start

Reality: The YouTube landscape is constantly evolving, creating new opportunities for creators. While competition has increased, so has the overall audience and the diversity of content niches.

Reasons it's not too late:
- New trends and topics emerge regularly
- Improvements in discovery algorithms help surface quality content
- Niche audiences are always looking for fresh perspectives
- Established creators may leave, creating gaps in the market

5. Conclusion

The YouTube gold rush is far from over. With its massive user base, diverse content landscape, and multiple revenue streams, YouTube continues to offer significant opportunities for content creators. By understanding the current platform dynamics, recognizing its financial potential, and avoiding common misconceptions, aspiring YouTubers can position themselves for success.

Remember, building a successful YouTube channel takes time, effort, and persistence. Focus on creating value for your audience, stay consistent, and be open to learning and adapting as you grow. With dedication and the right approach, you can tap into the ongoing YouTube gold rush and build a thriving channel.

CHAPTER 2: BUILDING YOUR YOUTUBE FOUNDATION

Points Covered

1. Introduction
2. Defining Your Niche and Target Audience
2.1. Understanding the Importance of a Niche
2.2. Identifying Your Target Audience
2.3. Researching Your Competition
3. Creating a Compelling Channel Identity
3.1. Developing Your Channel Name
3.2. Designing Your Channel Logo and Banner
3.3. Crafting Your Channel Description
4. Setting Up Your Channel for Optimal Performance
4.1. Customizing Your Channel Layout
4.2. Creating Playlists
4.3. Optimizing Your Video Titles and Descriptions
5. Conclusion

1. Introduction

In this chapter, we will explore the essential steps to build a strong foundation for your YouTube channel. By focusing on defining your niche, creating a compelling channel identity, and optimizing your channel setup, you'll be well-positioned to attract and retain viewers, setting the stage for long-term success on the platform.

2. Defining Your Niche and Target Audience

2.1. Understanding the Importance of a Niche

Choosing a specific niche for your YouTube channel is crucial for success. A niche allows you to:

- Stand out in a crowded market
- Build expertise in a particular area
- Attract a dedicated audience
- Create focused, high-quality content

To select your niche, consider your passions, skills, and knowledge. What topics can you talk about for hours? What unique perspective can you bring to the table?

2.2. Identifying Your Target Audience

Once you've chosen your niche, it's time to identify your target audience. Understanding who you're creating content for will help you tailor your videos to their needs and interests. Consider the following factors:

- Age range
- Gender
- Location
- Interests
- Pain points or challenges they face

Create a detailed viewer persona to guide your content creation process. This will help you craft videos that resonate with your audience and keep them coming back for more.

2.3. Researching Your Competition

Before finalizing your niche and target audience, take some time to research your competition. Look for other YouTube channels in

your chosen niche and ask yourself:
- What type of content are they creating?
- How often do they upload?
- What engagement levels do their videos receive?
- What gaps or opportunities can you identify?

Use this information to refine your niche and find ways to differentiate yourself from existing channels.

3. Creating a Compelling Channel Identity

3.1. Developing Your Channel Name

Your channel name is often the first thing potential viewers will see, so it's important to choose wisely. Consider these tips when selecting a name:
- Make it memorable and easy to spell
- Ensure it reflects your niche and content
- Check for availability across social media platforms
- Avoid using trademarked terms or names

Brainstorm several options and ask for feedback from friends or family before making your final decision.

3.2. Designing Your Channel Logo and Banner

Visual branding plays a significant role in creating a professional and cohesive channel identity. Your logo and banner should:
- Reflect your channel's personality and niche
- Use consistent colors and fonts
- Be easily recognizable at different sizes
- Include your channel name or tagline

If you're not confident in your design skills, consider hiring a freelance designer or using user-friendly design tools like Canva to create your visuals.

3.3. Crafting Your Channel Description

Your channel description is an opportunity to tell potential subscribers what your channel is all about. Write a clear and

concise description that:
- Explains your channel's purpose and the value you provide
- Highlights your upload schedule
- Includes relevant keywords for better searchability
- Showcases your personality and unique selling points

Remember to update your description regularly as your channel evolves and grows.

4. Setting Up Your Channel for Optimal Performance

4.1. Customizing Your Channel Layout

A well-organized channel layout helps viewers navigate your content easily. Take advantage of YouTube's customization options to:
- Feature your most popular or recent uploads
- Showcase different playlists or series
- Highlight your channel trailer for new visitors

Regularly review and update your layout to ensure it accurately represents your current content and goals.

4.2. Creating Playlists

Playlists are an excellent way to organize your content and keep viewers engaged. Consider creating playlists that:
- Group videos by topic or theme
- Showcase a series or multi-part content
- Highlight your best or most popular videos

Use clear and descriptive titles for your playlists to make them easily discoverable by both viewers and YouTube's algorithm.

4.3. Optimizing Your Video Titles and Descriptions

To improve your videos' visibility in search results and suggested videos, pay attention to your titles and descriptions. Follow these best practices:

- Use relevant keywords in your titles and descriptions
- Write clear, compelling titles that accurately describe your content
- Include a brief summary of your video in the first few lines of the description
- Add timestamps for longer videos to help viewers navigate to specific sections
- Include links to your social media profiles and other relevant resources

Remember to strike a balance between optimization and natural language. Your titles and descriptions should be informative and engaging for both viewers and search algorithms.

5. Conclusion

Building a strong foundation for your YouTube channel is essential for long-term success on the platform. By defining your niche and target audience, creating a compelling channel identity, and optimizing your channel setup, you'll be well-positioned to attract and retain viewers.

Remember that building a successful YouTube channel takes time and effort. Stay consistent with your content creation, engage with your audience, and be open to learning and adapting as you grow. With dedication and perseverance, you'll be on your way to achieving your YouTube goals.

CHAPTER 3: CONTENT CREATION STRATEGIES

Points Covered
1. Introduction
2. Developing a Content Calendar
2.1. Understanding the Importance of a Content Calendar
2.2. Steps to Create an Effective Content Calendar
2.3. Tools for Managing Your Content Calendar
3. Crafting Engaging and Shareable Videos
3.1. Elements of Engaging Video Content
3.2. Tips for Creating Shareable Videos
3.3. Video Editing Techniques
4. Implementing SEO Techniques for YouTube
4.1. Optimizing Video Titles and Descriptions
4.2. Using Tags and Categories Effectively
4.3. Creating Custom Thumbnails
4.4. Leveraging Playlists and End Screens
5. Conclusion

1. Introduction

In this chapter, we'll explore essential content creation strategies for YouTube success. We'll cover three main areas: developing a content calendar, crafting engaging and shareable videos, and implementing SEO techniques specifically for YouTube. These strategies will help you create a strong foundation for your

YouTube channel and increase your chances of success on the platform.

2. Developing a Content Calendar

2.1. Understanding the Importance of a Content Calendar

A content calendar is a powerful tool that helps you plan, organize, and schedule your YouTube videos. It allows you to:

- Maintain a consistent posting schedule
- Plan content in advance
- Align your videos with important dates or events
- Ensure a good mix of content types
- Collaborate more effectively with team members

2.2. Steps to Create an Effective Content Calendar

1. Define your content goals and target audience
2. Decide on your posting frequency
3. Brainstorm video ideas and themes
4. Categorize your content types
5. Plan your content around important dates or events
6. Assign responsibilities to team members
7. Set deadlines for each stage of video production
8. Review and adjust your calendar regularly

2.3. Tools for Managing Your Content Calendar

Several tools can help you create and manage your content calendar:

- Google Sheets or Excel: Simple and customizable
- Trello: Visual organization with boards and cards
- Asana: Project management tool with calendar view
- CoSchedule: Specifically designed for content marketing
- Airtable: Flexible database-style organization

Choose a tool that fits your needs and workflow, and make sure all team members have access to it.

3. Crafting Engaging and Shareable Videos

3.1. Elements of Engaging Video Content

To create videos that capture and hold your audience's attention:
- Start with a strong hook in the first few seconds
- Tell a compelling story or provide clear value
- Use high-quality visuals and audio
- Keep your content focused and concise
- Include a clear call-to-action

3.2. Tips for Creating Shareable Videos

To increase the likelihood of your videos being shared:
- Create content that evokes emotion
- Address current trends or hot topics
- Provide unique insights or perspectives
- Use humor when appropriate
- Make your videos easy to understand and share
- Encourage viewers to share in your video and description

3.3. Video Editing Techniques

Improve the quality of your videos with these editing techniques:
- Use cuts to maintain a good pace
- Add text overlays for key points
- Include background music to set the mood
- Use transitions sparingly and purposefully
- Color grade your footage for a consistent look
- Add graphics or animations to illustrate concepts

4. Implementing SEO Techniques for YouTube

4.1. Optimizing Video Titles and Descriptions

- Use keywords naturally in your titles

- Keep titles under 60 characters for full display in search results
- Write detailed, keyword-rich descriptions
- Include links to your website or social media in descriptions
- Add timestamps for longer videos

4.2. Using Tags and Categories Effectively

- Use relevant tags that accurately describe your video
- Include a mix of broad and specific tags
- Research popular tags in your niche
- Choose the most appropriate category for your video

4.3. Creating Custom Thumbnails

- Design eye-catching thumbnails that represent your video content
- Use high-contrast colors and clear text
- Include your branding elements
- Ensure thumbnails are clear when viewed at small sizes

4.4. Leveraging Playlists and End Screens

- Create themed playlists to group related videos
- Use end screens to promote other videos or playlists
- Encourage viewers to subscribe through end screens
- Link to your website or merchandise in end screens

5. Conclusion

By implementing these content creation strategies, you'll be well-equipped to grow your YouTube channel and engage your audience effectively. Remember to consistently apply these techniques, analyze your results, and adapt your approach as needed. With dedication and the right strategies, you can build a successful presence on YouTube and achieve your content creation goals.

CHAPTER 4: MASTERING YOUTUBE ANALYTICS

Points Covered

1. Introduction to YouTube Analytics
2. Key Metrics and Data Interpretation

2.1 Views and Watch Time
2.2 Audience Retention
2.3 Traffic Sources
2.4 Engagement Metrics

3. Using Analytics to Refine Content Strategy

3.1 Identifying Top-Performing Content
3.2 Optimizing Video Titles and Descriptions
3.3 Improving Thumbnails
3.4 Analyzing Upload Frequency and Timing

4. Leveraging Audience Insights for Growth

4.1 Understanding Audience Demographics
4.2 Identifying Viewer Preferences
4.3 Expanding Reach to New Audiences
4.4 Building a Community

5. Conclusion

1. Introduction to YouTube Analytics

CHAPTER 4: MASTERING YOUTUBE ANALYTICS

YouTube Analytics is a powerful tool that provides content creators with valuable insights into their channel's performance. By understanding and using this data effectively, you can make informed decisions to improve your content and grow your channel. In this chapter, we'll explore how to interpret key metrics, use analytics to refine your content strategy, and leverage audience insights for growth.

2. Key Metrics and Data Interpretation

2.1 Views and Watch Time

Views and watch time are two fundamental metrics that indicate the reach and engagement of your videos. While views show how many times your video has been watched, watch time reveals how long viewers spend watching your content. A high number of views with low watch time might suggest that your content isn't meeting viewer expectations or keeping them engaged.

2.2 Audience Retention

Audience retention shows how long viewers watch your videos before dropping off. This metric helps you understand which parts of your videos are most engaging and where viewers lose interest. By analyzing audience retention graphs, you can identify patterns and adjust your content to keep viewers watching longer.

2.3 Traffic Sources

Traffic sources reveal how viewers are finding your videos. This information can help you focus your promotion efforts on the most effective channels. Common traffic sources include YouTube search, suggested videos, external websites, and social media platforms.

2.4 Engagement Metrics

Engagement metrics include likes, dislikes, comments, and shares. These indicators show how viewers are interacting with your content. High engagement often correlates with better performance in YouTube's algorithm, leading to increased visibility for your videos.

3. Using Analytics to Refine Content Strategy

3.1 Identifying Top-Performing Content

By analyzing your most successful videos, you can identify common themes, formats, or topics that resonate with your audience. Use this information to create more content that aligns with what your viewers enjoy.

3.2 Optimizing Video Titles and Descriptions

Look at the search terms that lead viewers to your videos. Use this data to improve your video titles and descriptions, incorporating relevant keywords to increase your visibility in search results.

3.3 Improving Thumbnails

Compare the click-through rates of different thumbnails to determine which styles are most effective at attracting viewers. Use this information to create eye-catching thumbnails that encourage clicks.

3.4 Analyzing Upload Frequency and Timing

Study when your audience is most active and adjust your upload schedule accordingly. Experiment with different posting frequencies to find the right balance between consistency and quality.

4. Leveraging Audience Insights for Growth

4.1 Understanding Audience Demographics

YouTube provides information about your viewers' age, gender, and location. Use this data to tailor your content to your audience's preferences and create videos that appeal to your core demographic.

4.2 Identifying Viewer Preferences

Analyze which topics, video lengths, and formats perform best with your audience. This information can guide your content creation process and help you produce videos that your viewers will enjoy and share.

4.3 Expanding Reach to New Audiences
Use audience overlap reports to identify other channels and topics that interest your viewers. This can help you find collaboration opportunities and new content ideas that may attract a broader audience.

4.4 Building a Community
Pay attention to comments and community posts to understand what your audience wants to see. Engage with your viewers by responding to comments and creating content that addresses their questions and suggestions.

5. Conclusion
Mastering YouTube Analytics is essential for any content creator looking to grow their channel and improve their videos. By interpreting key metrics, refining your content strategy based on data, and leveraging audience insights, you can make informed decisions that will help your channel thrive.

Remember that analytics should guide your decisions, not dictate them entirely. Always balance data-driven insights with your creative vision and passion for your content. With practice and persistence, you'll become adept at using YouTube Analytics to create videos that resonate with your audience and help your channel grow.

CHAPTER 5: MONETIZATION METHODS BEYOND ADSENSE

Points Covered

1. Introduction
2. Exploring Sponsorships and Brand Deals
2.1. Understanding Sponsorships
2.2. Finding the Right Brand Partnerships
2.3. Negotiating Sponsorship Deals
3. Implementing Affiliate Marketing Strategies
3.1. What is Affiliate Marketing?
3.2. Choosing the Right Affiliate Programs
3.3. Effective Affiliate Marketing Techniques
4. Creating and Selling Digital Products
4.1. Types of Digital Products
4.2. Developing Your Digital Product
4.3. Marketing and Selling Your Digital Products
5. Conclusion

1. Introduction

In today's online world, content creators and businesses have many options to make money beyond traditional advertising methods like AdSense. This chapter explores three powerful monetization strategies: sponsorships and brand deals, affiliate marketing, and creating and selling digital products. By understanding and using these methods, you can increase your income and build a stronger, more diverse business.

2. Exploring Sponsorships and Brand Deals

2.1. Understanding Sponsorships

Sponsorships are partnerships where a company pays you to promote their products or services to your audience. These deals can be a great way to earn money while providing value to your followers. Sponsorships can take many forms, such as:

- Sponsored content (blog posts, videos, social media posts)
- Product reviews
- Brand ambassador programs
- Event sponsorships

2.2. Finding the Right Brand Partnerships

To find sponsorship opportunities that fit your brand and audience:

1. Know your audience: Understand their interests, needs, and demographics.
2. Research potential partners: Look for brands that align with your values and audience interests.
3. Build your platform: Grow your following and engagement to attract sponsors.
4. Network: Attend industry events and connect with brands on social media.
5. Use sponsorship platforms: Websites like AspireIQ and Grapevine Logic can connect you with brands.

2.3. Negotiating Sponsorship Deals

When negotiating sponsorship deals:

1. Know your worth: Research industry rates and set fair prices for your work.
2. Be clear about deliverables: Outline exactly what you'll provide in the partnership.
3. Maintain authenticity: Only work with brands you genuinely believe in.
4. Discuss terms: Agree on payment schedules, content approval processes, and exclusivity clauses.
5. Get it in writing: Always use a contract to protect both parties.

3. Implementing Affiliate Marketing Strategies

3.1. What is Affiliate Marketing?

Affiliate marketing is a system where you earn a commission for promoting other people's or companies' products. When someone buys a product through your unique affiliate link, you get a percentage of the sale.

3.2. Choosing the Right Affiliate Programs

To select the best affiliate programs for your business:

1. Choose products relevant to your niche and audience.
2. Look for programs with fair commission rates (typically 5-30%).
3. Consider the reputation of the company and product quality.
4. Check the cookie duration (how long you'll earn commissions after someone clicks your link).
5. Evaluate the support and resources provided by the affiliate program.

Some popular affiliate networks include Amazon Associates, ShareASale, and CJ Affiliate.

3.3. Effective Affiliate Marketing Techniques

To succeed in affiliate marketing:
1. Create valuable content: Write honest reviews, comparisons, and how-to guides.
2. Disclose your affiliate relationships: Be transparent with your audience about your partnerships.
3. Use multiple promotion channels: Incorporate affiliate links in blog posts, emails, social media, and videos.
4. Track your results: Use analytics to see which products and strategies perform best.
5. Test different approaches: Try various call-to-action phrases and placements to optimize conversions.

4. Creating and Selling Digital Products

4.1. Types of Digital Products

Digital products are items that can be sold and delivered online. Some popular types include:
- E-books and PDF guides
- Online courses and workshops
- Templates and printables
- Software and apps
- Digital art and designs
- Music and audio files

4.2. Developing Your Digital Product

To create a successful digital product:
1. Identify a need: Solve a problem or fulfill a desire for your target audience.
2. Research the market: Ensure there's demand for your product and study competitors.
3. Plan your content: Outline your product and decide on the format.
4. Create high-quality content: Invest time in developing valuable, well-designed products.

5. Set up a delivery system: Choose a platform to host and deliver your digital products.

4.3. Marketing and Selling Your Digital Products

To effectively sell your digital products:

1. Build an email list: Use lead magnets to gather potential customers' contact information.
2. Create a sales page: Highlight the benefits of your product and include customer testimonials.
3. Use content marketing: Write blog posts, create videos, or host webinars related to your product.
4. Leverage social media: Share snippets of your product and engage with your audience.
5. Offer limited-time promotions: Create urgency with special deals or launch discounts.
6. Provide excellent customer support: Address questions and concerns promptly to build trust.

5. Conclusion

By exploring sponsorships and brand deals, implementing affiliate marketing strategies, and creating and selling digital products, you can significantly increase your income beyond AdSense. These monetization methods offer flexibility and scalability, allowing you to grow your business and reach new audiences. Remember to stay authentic, provide value to your audience, and continuously test and refine your approach to find the best combination of strategies for your unique situation. With dedication and smart planning, you can build a thriving online business using these diverse monetization methods.

CHAPTER 6: BUILDING A LOYAL COMMUNITY

Points Covered
1. Introduction
2. Engaging with Your Audience Effectively
2.1. Understanding Your Audience
2.2. Creating Engaging Content
2.3. Responding to Comments and Feedback
3. Developing a Strong Brand Personality
3.1. Defining Your Brand Values
3.2. Creating a Consistent Voice
3.3. Showcasing Your Unique Style
4. Leveraging Community Features on YouTube
4.1. Using Community Posts
4.2. Implementing Live Streams
4.3. Creating Polls and Surveys
5. Conclusion

1. Introduction

Building a loyal community is crucial for the success of your YouTube channel. This chapter will guide you through effective strategies to engage with your audience, develop a strong brand personality, and make the most of YouTube's community features. By implementing these techniques, you'll create a dedicated following that supports your channel's growth and success.

2. Engaging with Your Audience Effectively

2.1. Understanding Your Audience

To engage effectively with your audience, you must first understand who they are. Take time to analyze your channel's demographics, viewing habits, and preferences. Use YouTube Analytics to gather data on your viewers' age, location, and interests. This information will help you tailor your content and communication style to better suit your audience's needs and expectations.

2.2. Creating Engaging Content

Producing content that resonates with your audience is key to building a loyal community. Consider the following tips:

- Focus on topics that interest your viewers
- Use eye-catching thumbnails and titles
- Keep your videos well-paced and informative
- Include calls-to-action that encourage viewer participation
- Create series or themed content to keep viewers coming back

Remember to maintain a balance between consistency and variety in your content to keep your audience engaged and excited about your channel.

2.3. Responding to Comments and Feedback

Actively engaging with your viewers through comments is a powerful way to build a strong community. Make it a habit to:

- Respond to comments promptly and thoughtfully
- Address questions and concerns
- Thank viewers for their support and feedback
- Encourage discussions among your community members

By showing that you value your audience's input, you'll foster a sense of belonging and loyalty among your viewers.

3. Developing a Strong Brand Personality

3.1. Defining Your Brand Values

Your brand values are the core principles that guide your channel's content and interactions. Take time to identify and articulate these values clearly. Consider what makes your channel unique and what message you want to convey to your audience. Your brand values should be evident in every aspect of your channel, from your content to your community interactions.

3.2. Creating a Consistent Voice

Consistency in your communication style helps viewers connect with your brand on a personal level. Develop a voice that reflects your brand personality and use it consistently across all platforms, including:

- Video content
- Video descriptions
- Social media posts
- Community posts
- Responses to comments

Whether your brand voice is friendly, professional, or humorous, maintain it throughout all your interactions to build a strong and recognizable brand identity.

3.3. Showcasing Your Unique Style

Your channel's visual elements play a significant role in defining your brand personality. Create a cohesive look for your channel by:

- Designing a memorable channel icon and banner
- Using consistent color schemes and fonts
- Creating custom thumbnails that reflect your brand style
- Developing a unique intro or outro for your videos

These visual cues will help viewers instantly recognize your content and strengthen your brand identity.

4. Leveraging Community Features on YouTube

4.1. Using Community Posts

Community posts are a valuable tool for engaging with your audience between video uploads. Use them to:

- Share updates and announcements
- Post behind-the-scenes content
- Ask for viewer opinions or suggestions
- Share relevant links or resources

Regular community posts keep your audience engaged and provide additional value beyond your video content.

4.2. Implementing Live Streams

Live streams offer a unique opportunity to interact with your audience in real-time. Consider hosting regular live streams to:

- Answer viewer questions
- Provide live tutorials or demonstrations
- Discuss current events or topics relevant to your niche
- Host Q&A sessions or AMAs (Ask Me Anything)

Live streams create a sense of immediacy and personal connection that can significantly strengthen your community bonds.

4.3. Creating Polls and Surveys

Polls and surveys are excellent tools for gathering viewer feedback and involving your audience in your channel's direction. Use them to:

- Ask for content suggestions
- Get opinions on potential video topics
- Understand viewer preferences
- Encourage audience participation in decision-making

By involving your viewers in these processes, you make them feel valued and invested in your channel's success.

5. Conclusion

Building a loyal community on YouTube requires consistent effort and genuine engagement with your audience. By understanding your viewers, creating engaging content, developing a strong brand personality, and making the most of YouTube's community features, you'll create a supportive and active community around your channel. Remember that community-building is an ongoing process, and your efforts will pay off in the form of a dedicated audience that supports your channel's growth and success.

CHAPTER 7: COLLABORATIONS AND NETWORKING

Points Covered

1. Introduction
2. Finding Potential Collaborators
2.1. Research and Identify
2.2. Evaluate Compatibility
2.3. Reach Out and Connect
3. Approaching Potential Collaborators
3.1. Crafting Your Pitch
3.2. Making the First Contact
3.3. Following Up
4. Maximizing the Benefits of Cross-Promotion
4.1. Understanding Cross-Promotion
4.2. Planning Collaborative Content
4.3. Promoting Each Other's Channels
4.4. Measuring Success
5. Building Relationships within the YouTube Community
5.1. Engaging with Other Creators
5.2. Participating in YouTube Events
5.3. Joining YouTube Groups and Forums

    5.4. Giving Back to the Community
    6. Conclusion

1. Introduction

In the world of YouTube, collaborations and networking play a crucial role in growing your channel and expanding your audience. This chapter will guide you through the process of finding and approaching potential collaborators, making the most of cross-promotion opportunities, and building lasting relationships within the YouTube community.

2. Finding Potential Collaborators

2.1. Research and Identify

To find potential collaborators, start by researching creators in your niche or related areas. Look for channels with similar content themes, audience demographics, or complementary skills. Use YouTube's search function, explore suggested channels, and browse trending videos in your category to discover potential partners.

2.2. Evaluate Compatibility

Once you've identified potential collaborators, assess their channel to ensure compatibility. Consider factors such as:

- Channel size and subscriber count
- Content quality and style
- Audience engagement levels
- Brand values and messaging

Aim for collaborators who have a similar or slightly larger audience than yours, as this can lead to mutually beneficial partnerships.

2.3. Reach Out and Connect

Before making a formal collaboration request, start building a relationship with potential partners. Follow their channel, watch their videos, and engage with their content by leaving thoughtful comments. This approach helps you get noticed and lays the groundwork for future collaboration.

3. Approaching Potential Collaborators

3.1. Crafting Your Pitch

When you're ready to propose a collaboration, prepare a clear and compelling pitch. Your pitch should include:

- A brief introduction of yourself and your channel
- Why you're interested in collaborating with them
- Your idea for the collaboration
- The benefits for both parties
- Your contact information

Keep your pitch concise, friendly, and professional.

3.2. Making the First Contact

Choose the most appropriate method to reach out to your potential collaborator. Options include:

- Email (if available on their channel or website)
- YouTube's messaging system
- Social media platforms

Personalize your message and show that you've done your research on their channel.

3.3. Following Up

If you don't receive a response within a week or two, it's okay to send a polite follow-up message. Remember that popular creators may receive many collaboration requests, so be patient and respectful of their time.

4. Maximizing the Benefits of Cross-Promotion

4.1. Understanding Cross-Promotion

Cross-promotion involves creators working together to promote each other's content to their respective audiences. This strategy can help both parties gain new subscribers and increase visibility.

4.2. Planning Collaborative Content

When planning a collaboration, consider content ideas that will appeal to both your audiences. Some popular collaboration formats include:

- Guest appearances in each other's videos
- Joint live streams or Q&A sessions
- Challenges or competitions
- Collaborative series or projects

Ensure that the content aligns with both channels' themes and styles.

4.3. Promoting Each Other's Channels

To make the most of your collaboration, actively promote your partner's channel to your audience. This can include:

- Mentioning them in your videos
- Adding links to their channel in your video descriptions
- Sharing their content on your social media platforms
- Creating teaser content to build excitement for the collaboration

4.4. Measuring Success

After your collaboration, assess its impact on both channels. Look at metrics such as:

- Subscriber growth
- View counts on collaborative videos
- Engagement rates (likes, comments, shares)
- Cross-traffic between channels

Use these insights to refine your approach for future collaborations.

5. Building Relationships within the YouTube Community

5.1. Engaging with Other Creators

Building relationships goes beyond formal collaborations.

Regularly engage with other creators in your niche by:
- Commenting on their videos
- Sharing their content on social media
- Mentioning their work in your videos when relevant

This ongoing engagement helps you stay connected and increases the likelihood of future collaborations.

5.2. Participating in YouTube Events

Take part in YouTube-specific events to network with other creators and industry professionals. These events can include:
- VidCon and other creator conferences
- YouTube-sponsored workshops and meetups
- Online creator events and webinars

These gatherings provide opportunities to learn, share experiences, and make valuable connections.

5.3. Joining YouTube Groups and Forums

Become an active member of YouTube communities and forums. Participate in discussions, offer advice, and seek help when needed. Some popular platforms include:
- Reddit's YouTube-related subreddits
- Facebook groups for YouTube creators
- Discord servers focused on content creation

These communities can be great sources of support, inspiration, and potential collaborations.

5.4. Giving Back to the Community

As you grow your channel, look for ways to support other creators, especially those who are just starting. This can include:
- Offering advice and tips in community forums
- Featuring smaller channels in your content
- Providing constructive feedback on others' videos

By supporting others, you build a positive reputation within the community and foster goodwill that can lead to future opportunities.

6. Conclusion

Collaborations and networking are powerful tools for growing your YouTube channel and building a supportive community. By actively seeking out partnerships, maximizing cross-promotion opportunities, and nurturing relationships within the YouTube ecosystem, you can accelerate your channel's growth and create a more enjoyable and rewarding experience as a content creator. Remember that building strong connections takes time and effort, but the long-term benefits for your channel and career are well worth the investment.

CHAPTER 8: SCALING YOUR YOUTUBE BUSINESS

Points Covered

1. Introduction
2. Hiring and Managing a Team
2.1. Identifying Roles
2.2. Recruitment Process
2.3. Team Management
3. Streamlining Your Production Process
3.1. Analyzing Current Workflow
3.2. Implementing Efficient Systems
3.3. Utilizing Technology
4. Expanding to Multiple Channels or Platforms
4.1. Assessing New Opportunities
4.2. Developing a Multi-Platform Strategy
4.3. Managing Cross-Platform Content
5. Conclusion

1. Introduction

As your YouTube business grows, you'll face new challenges and opportunities. This chapter focuses on three key areas that will help you scale your operations: building a team, improving your production process, and expanding to new platforms. By mastering these aspects, you'll be well-positioned to take your YouTube business to the next level.

2. Hiring and Managing a Team

2.1. Identifying Roles

To scale your YouTube business, you'll need to bring in additional talent. Start by identifying the roles that will have the biggest impact on your channel's growth. Common positions include:

- Video editors
- Graphic designers
- Script writers
- Researchers
- Social media managers
- Administrative assistants

Determine which roles are most critical for your channel's success and prioritize hiring for those positions first.

2.2. Recruitment Process

Once you've identified the roles you need to fill, it's time to start the recruitment process. Here are some steps to follow:

1. Write clear job descriptions outlining responsibilities and required skills.
2. Post job listings on relevant platforms (e.g., job boards, social media, industry forums).
3. Review applications and portfolios.
4. Conduct interviews with promising candidates.
5. Assign test projects to assess skills and fit.
6. Make job offers to the best candidates.

Remember to look for individuals who not only have the necessary skills but also fit well with your channel's culture and vision.

2.3. Team Management

Managing a team requires different skills than running a solo operation. Here are some tips for effective team management:
- Set clear expectations and goals for each team member.
- Establish regular communication channels (e.g., team meetings, project management tools).
- Provide constructive feedback and recognition for good work.
- Foster a positive work environment that encourages creativity and collaboration.
- Invest in your team's growth through training and development opportunities.

By building a strong, motivated team, you'll be able to produce higher-quality content more consistently, helping your channel grow faster.

3. Streamlining Your Production Process

3.1. Analyzing Current Workflow

To improve your production process, start by examining your current workflow. Identify bottlenecks, inefficiencies, and areas where quality might be compromised. Ask yourself and your team:
- Which tasks take the most time?
- Are there any repetitive tasks that could be automated?
- Where do errors or quality issues most often occur?
- Are there any communication breakdowns in the process?

Use this analysis to prioritize areas for improvement.

3.2. Implementing Efficient Systems

Based on your workflow analysis, implement new systems to increase efficiency:

1. Create templates for scripts, thumbnails, and video descriptions.
2. Develop a content calendar to plan and schedule videos

in advance.
3. Establish a clear review and approval process for each stage of production.
4. Set up a file organization system for easy access to assets and completed projects.
5. Use project management tools to track progress and deadlines.

These systems will help streamline your workflow and ensure consistency across your content.

3.3. Utilizing Technology

Leverage technology to further improve your production process:

- Invest in high-quality equipment (cameras, microphones, lighting) to reduce setup time and improve output.
- Use editing software with time-saving features like keyboard shortcuts and presets.
- Implement cloud storage solutions for easy file sharing and collaboration.
- Explore AI tools for tasks like transcription or basic editing.

By embracing technology, you can significantly speed up your production process without sacrificing quality.

4. Expanding to Multiple Channels or Platforms

4.1. Assessing New Opportunities

As your YouTube channel grows, you may want to explore other platforms to reach new audiences. Consider these factors when assessing new opportunities:

- Audience demographics and preferences
- Platform-specific content requirements
- Monetization options

- Time and resources needed to create platform-specific content
- Potential for cross-promotion with your YouTube channel

Research thoroughly and start with one or two new platforms that align best with your content and target audience.

4.2. Developing a Multi-Platform Strategy

To successfully expand to new platforms, develop a clear strategy:

1. Set specific goals for each platform (e.g., audience growth, engagement, revenue).
2. Tailor your content to fit each platform's unique features and audience expectations.
3. Create a content calendar that balances output across all platforms.
4. Develop a consistent brand voice and visual identity across platforms.
5. Plan for cross-promotion to drive traffic between your various channels.

Remember that each platform may require a slightly different approach, so be prepared to adapt your strategy as you learn what works best.

4.3. Managing Cross-Platform Content

Efficiently managing content across multiple platforms is key to successful expansion:

- Repurpose content when possible (e.g., turning YouTube videos into shorter clips for TikTok or Instagram).
- Use scheduling tools to plan and post content across platforms.
- Monitor performance on each platform and adjust your strategy accordingly.
- Engage with your audience consistently across all platforms.

- Consider hiring platform-specific managers as your presence grows.

By effectively managing your cross-platform content, you can maximize your reach and engagement without overwhelming your team.

5. Conclusion

Scaling your YouTube business requires careful planning and execution. By building a strong team, streamlining your production process, and expanding to new platforms, you'll be well-positioned for long-term growth and success. Remember that scaling is an ongoing process – continuously evaluate your progress, adapt to changes, and stay focused on creating value for your audience. With persistence and smart strategies, you can take your YouTube business to new heights.

CHAPTER 9: ADVANCED MONETIZATION TECHNIQUES

Points Covered

1. Introduction
2. Creating and Monetizing a Membership Community
2.1. Defining Your Community
2.2. Setting Up Your Membership Platform
2.3. Pricing Strategies
2.4. Engaging and Retaining Members
3. Leveraging YouTube Shorts for Additional Revenue
3.1. Understanding YouTube Shorts
3.2. Creating Engaging Shorts Content
3.3. Monetization Options for Shorts
3.4. Promoting Your Shorts
4. Exploring Opportunities in YouTube's Partner Programs
4.1. YouTube Partner Program Overview
4.2. Eligibility Requirements
4.3. Monetization Features
4.4. Maximizing Your Earnings

5. Conclusion

1. Introduction

In this chapter, we'll dive into advanced monetization techniques that can help you take your YouTube channel to the next level. We'll explore three key areas: creating and monetizing a membership community, leveraging YouTube Shorts for additional revenue, and making the most of YouTube's partner programs. These strategies will help you diversify your income streams and grow your channel's profitability.

2. Creating and Monetizing a Membership Community

2.1. Defining Your Community

To create a successful membership community, you need to understand your audience and what they value. Consider the following:

- Identify your target audience
- Determine what unique value you can offer
- Define the goals of your community

2.2. Setting Up Your Membership Platform

Choose a platform that suits your needs and your audience's preferences. Options include:

- YouTube's built-in membership feature
- Third-party platforms like Patreon or Memberful
- Custom website with membership functionality

2.3. Pricing Strategies

Develop a pricing strategy that reflects the value you provide and aligns with your audience's expectations:

- Tiered membership levels with different benefits
- Monthly vs. annual subscription options
- Early bird or promotional pricing to encourage sign-ups

2.4. Engaging and Retaining Members

Keep your community active and engaged to reduce churn:
- Regular exclusive content
- Live Q&A sessions or workshops
- Community challenges or events
- Personalized interaction with members

3. Leveraging YouTube Shorts for Additional Revenue

3.1. Understanding YouTube Shorts

YouTube Shorts are short-form vertical videos designed for mobile viewing:
- Maximum duration of 60 seconds
- Accessible through the Shorts shelf on YouTube
- Potential for viral growth and increased channel visibility

3.2. Creating Engaging Shorts Content

To make the most of Shorts, focus on creating content that:
- Captures attention quickly
- Provides value or entertainment in a short time
- Uses trending audio or popular Shorts features
- Encourages viewers to check out your long-form content

3.3. Monetization Options for Shorts

While direct monetization for Shorts is limited, you can use them to drive revenue indirectly:
- Shorts Fund: YouTube's initiative to reward creators for popular Shorts
- Driving traffic to your main channel and monetized videos
- Promoting products or services in your Shorts

3.4. Promoting Your Shorts

Increase the visibility of your Shorts to maximize their impact:

- Use relevant hashtags
- Share Shorts on other social media platforms
- Encourage viewers to subscribe and check out your main channel

4. Exploring Opportunities in YouTube's Partner Programs

4.1. YouTube Partner Program Overview

The YouTube Partner Program (YPP) allows creators to monetize their content through various features:

- Ad revenue sharing
- Channel memberships
- Super Chat and Super Stickers
- Merchandise shelf

4.2. Eligibility Requirements

To join the YPP, you need to meet certain criteria:

- 1,000 subscribers
- 4,000 watch hours in the past 12 months
- Compliance with YouTube's policies and guidelines
- An AdSense account linked to your channel

4.3. Monetization Features

Once you're in the YPP, you can access various monetization features:

- Ad revenue: Earn money from ads displayed on your videos
- Channel memberships: Offer paid subscriptions to your viewers
- Super Chat and Super Stickers: Allow viewers to pay to highlight their messages in live chats
- Merchandise shelf: Sell branded merchandise directly on your channel

4.4. Maximizing Your Earnings

To get the most out of the YPP:

- Create content that attracts high-value advertisers
- Encourage viewers to become channel members
- Promote your merchandise during videos and in video descriptions
- Use end screens and cards to direct viewers to other monetized content

5. Conclusion

By implementing these advanced monetization techniques, you can significantly increase your YouTube channel's revenue potential. Creating a membership community allows you to offer exclusive content and build a loyal fan base. Leveraging YouTube Shorts helps you reach new audiences and drive traffic to your main channel. Finally, making the most of YouTube's partner programs ensures you're taking advantage of all available monetization options. Remember, success on YouTube requires consistent effort, quality content, and a willingness to adapt to new opportunities and features.

CHAPTER 10: FROM YOUTUBER TO MILLIONAIRE

Points Covered

1. Introduction
2. Developing a Long-Term Growth Strategy

2.1 Setting Clear Goals

2.2 Understanding Your Audience

2.3 Creating a Content Calendar

2.4 Investing in Quality Equipment

3. Diversifying Your Income Streams

3.1 Advertising Revenue

3.2 Sponsorships and Brand Deals

3.3 Merchandise and Products

3.4 Patreon and Fan Funding

3.5 Affiliate Marketing

4. Building a Sustainable YouTube Empire

4.1 Consistency and Quality

4.2 Collaboration and Networking

4.3 Adapting to Platform Changes

4.4 Managing Your Finances

4.5 Building a Team

5. Conclusion

1. Introduction

Becoming a millionaire through YouTube is no longer just a dream. With the right strategy, dedication, and smart business decisions, you can turn your passion for creating content into a lucrative career. This chapter will guide you through the process of developing a long-term growth strategy, diversifying your income streams, and building a sustainable YouTube empire.

2. Developing a Long-Term Growth Strategy

2.1 Setting Clear Goals

To achieve success on YouTube, you need to have a clear vision of what you want to accomplish. Set specific, measurable, achievable, relevant, and time-bound (SMART) goals for your channel. These goals might include reaching a certain number of subscribers, achieving a specific view count, or earning a target income.

2.2 Understanding Your Audience

Knowing your audience is crucial for creating content that resonates with them. Use YouTube Analytics to gather insights about your viewers' demographics, interests, and viewing habits. This information will help you tailor your content to meet their needs and preferences.

2.3 Creating a Content Calendar

Plan your content in advance by creating a content calendar. This will help you maintain a consistent posting schedule and ensure that you're always prepared with fresh ideas. Include a mix of different video types, such as tutorials, vlogs, and collaborations, to keep your content varied and interesting.

2.4 Investing in Quality Equipment

While you don't need the most expensive gear to start, investing in good quality equipment can significantly improve the production value of your videos. Consider upgrading your camera, microphone, and editing software as your channel grows.

3. Diversifying Your Income Streams

3.1 Advertising Revenue

YouTube's Partner Program allows you to earn money through ads displayed on your videos. To maximize your advertising revenue, focus on creating engaging content that keeps viewers watching for longer periods.

3.2 Sponsorships and Brand Deals

As your channel grows, you'll have opportunities to work with brands on sponsored content. Be selective about the brands you partner with, ensuring they align with your values and your audience's interests.

3.3 Merchandise and Products

Create and sell your own merchandise, such as t-shirts, mugs, or other products related to your channel. This not only provides an additional income stream but also helps build brand loyalty among your fans.

3.4 Patreon and Fan Funding

Platforms like Patreon allow your most dedicated fans to support you directly through monthly contributions. In return, you can offer exclusive content or perks to these supporters.

3.5 Affiliate Marketing

Promote products or services in your videos and include affiliate links in your video descriptions. When viewers make purchases through these links, you earn a commission.

4. Building a Sustainable YouTube Empire

4.1 Consistency and Quality

Maintain a regular posting schedule and always strive to improve the quality of your content. Consistency builds trust with your audience, while high-quality content keeps them coming back for more.

4.2 Collaboration and Networking

Collaborate with other YouTubers in your niche to reach new audiences and learn from your peers. Attend industry events and conferences to network and stay up-to-date with the latest trends.

4.3 Adapting to Platform Changes

YouTube's algorithms and policies are constantly evolving. Stay informed about these changes and be ready to adapt your strategy accordingly to maintain your channel's growth and success.

4.4 Managing Your Finances

As your income grows, it's important to manage your finances wisely. Consider working with a financial advisor to help you make smart investment decisions and plan for the future.

4.5 Building a Team

As your channel expands, you may need to hire help to manage various aspects of your business. This could include editors, producers, or a manager to handle business inquiries.

5. Conclusion

Transforming your YouTube channel into a million-dollar business requires hard work, dedication, and smart planning. By developing a long-term growth strategy, diversifying your income streams, and building a sustainable empire, you can turn your passion for creating content into a successful and lucrative career. Remember, success doesn't happen overnight, but with persistence and the right approach, you can achieve your goals and become a YouTube millionaire.

ABOUT THE AUTHOR

Joe Ilunjo

Is a writer, a digital marketing expert and seasoned content creator with years of experience in helping brands and individuals succeed on YouTube. His passion for leveraging the power of online platforms has inspired him to write "YouTube Millionaire Blueprint", a step-by-step guide for creators looking to turn their creativity into income. Joe's approachable teaching style and deep understanding of YouTube's ever-evolving ecosystem have made him a sought-after consultant for both beginners and established creators. When he's not creating, Joe enjoys exploring new video trends, staying updated on the latest tech tools, and mentoring aspiring YouTubers.

www.ingramcontent.com/pod-product-compliance
Lightning Source LLC
Chambersburg PA
CBHW070419230526
45471CB00006B/2889